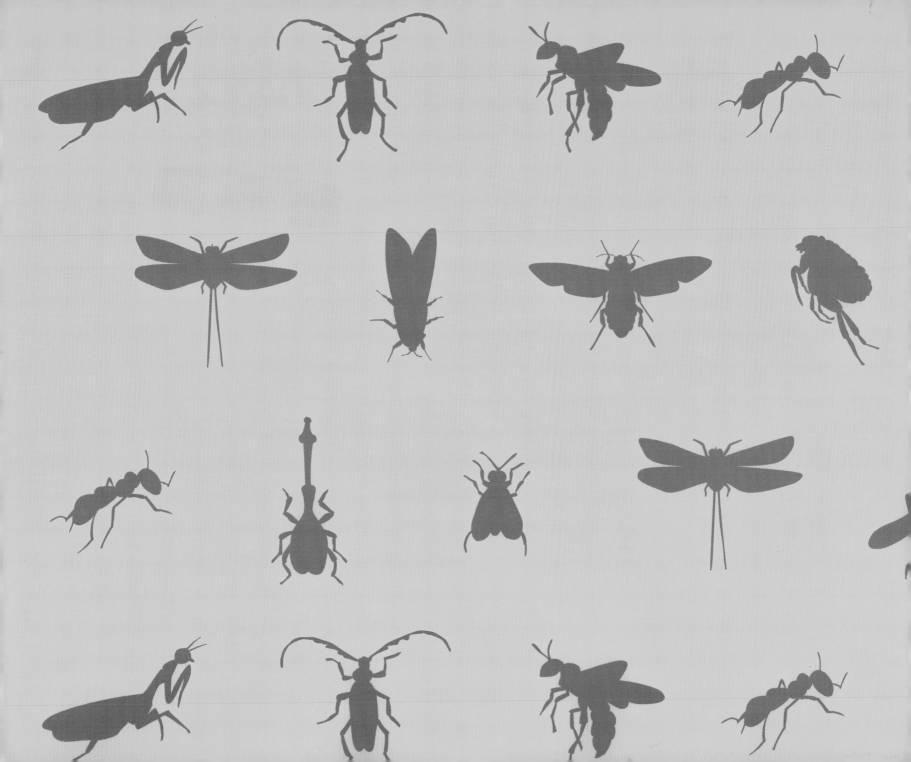

LET'S-READ-AND-FIND-OUT SCIENCE®

STAGE 1

Bugs Are Insects

by Anne Rockwell • illustrated by Steve Jenkins

HarperCollins Publishers

For Nicholas Alcorn and Christian Brion,
who have taught me a lot about looking at insects
—A.R.

For Jamie
—S.J.

Special thanks to Ed Spevak of Butterfly Kingdom
for his expert advice

The *Let's-Read-and-Find-Out Science* book series was originated
by Dr. Franklyn M. Branley, Astronomer Emeritus and former Chairman of the
American Museum–Hayden Planetarium, and was formerly co-edited by him and Dr. Roma Gans,
Professor Emeritus of Childhood Education, Teachers College, Columbia University.
Text and illustrations for each of the books in the series are checked for
accuracy by an expert in the relevant field. For more information about
Let's-Read-and-Find-Out Science books, write to HarperCollins Children's Books,
1350 Avenue of the Americas, New York, NY 10019,
or visit our website at www.letsreadandfindout.com.

HarperCollins® ®, and Let's-Read-and-Find-Out-Science® are trademarks of HarperCollins Publishers Inc.

Library of Congress Cataloging-in-Publication Data
Rockwell, Anne F.
Bugs are insects / by Anne Rockwell; illustrated by Steve Jenkins.
p.   cm.—(Let's-read-and-find-out. Stage 1)
Summary: Introduces common backyard insects and explains the basic characteristics of these creatures.
ISBN 0-06-028568-0—ISBN 0-06-028569-9 (lib. bdg.)—ISBN 0-06-445203-4 (pbk.)
1. Insects—Juvenile literature.   [1. Insects.]   I. Jenkins, Steve, 1952– ill.   II. Title.
III. Series.
QL467.2.R65   2001   99-39846
595.7—dc21

Typography by Elynn Cohen 11 12 13 14 15 16 17 18 19 20 ❖ First Edition

There are many kinds of insects living
all around us. Ants are insects.
So are crickets and mosquitoes.
So are butterflies and bees.

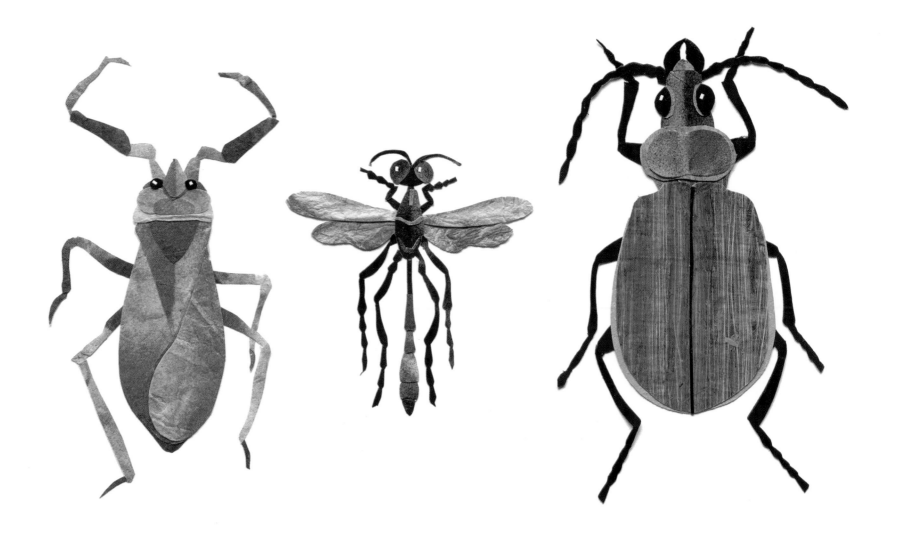

Insects come in many shapes, sizes, and colors. They don't all look alike, but there's a way to tell if something is an insect. Count its legs. Count how many parts make up its body.

Is a ladybug an insect?

All insects have external skeletons.

You have a hard skeleton *inside*, with parts that move. Your skeleton holds you up and helps give your body its shape. But an insect has a hard skeleton on the *outside*, with parts that move. The skeleton is like a shell around its body. It holds the insect up and gives its body its shape.

A ladybug has an external skeleton. Does that mean it's an insect?

Maybe not. All insects have external skeletons,
but not all animals with external skeletons are
insects. Crabs, lobsters, shrimps, and scorpions
have external skeletons too, but they are not insects.

Many insects have two pairs
of wings and a pair of antennae.
Sometimes the antennae are long,
like those of crickets or butterflies.
Sometimes they are short,
like those of beetles.

But all insect bodies are divided into three parts: head, thorax, and abdomen. There are six legs attached to the thorax. Anything that has six legs and three body parts is an insect.

A ladybug has six legs and three body parts. Is it an insect?

Now look at a spider. Is it an insect?

It has an external skeleton. But count its legs. How many does it have? Now count how many body parts it has.

A spider has eight legs, not six. Its body is divided into two parts, not three. So it is not an insect. A spider is an arachnid. Scorpions and daddy longlegs are arachnids too.

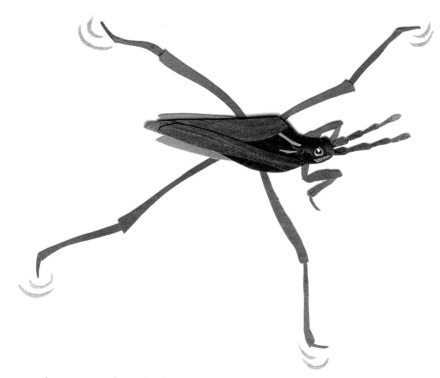

Now we know that a ladybug is an insect. But is it really a bug?

We sometimes call insects bugs. Many people think the two words mean the same thing, but they don't. A bug is an insect with a mouth like a beak and a head that forms a triangle. A stinkbug is a bug. So is a bedbug, and so is a water strider, even though it doesn't have the word "bug" in its name.

But a ladybug's mouth doesn't look like a beak. Its head isn't shaped like a triangle. A ladybug isn't a bug at all! It is a beetle. Beetles are insects with a pair of hard wings you can't see through that hides a second pair of clear wings. The hard wings make a straight line down the top of the abdomen when they are closed.

Different kinds of insects have different kinds of mouths to suck, pierce, bite, or chew. A mosquito has a mouth that can pierce your skin and draw blood. A butterfly has a long, curled-up mouth part for sucking nectar from flowers just like you suck juice through a straw.

22

Different kinds of insects have different kinds of legs as well. Crickets have long back legs for jumping. Water boatmen have wide, flat legs for paddling. Bees have fuzzy legs that can carry pollen from flower to flower. Grasshoppers have legs for making music.

Some insects are good builders. Ants build tunnels. Bees build honeycombs of wax that comes from their bodies. Wasps build paper nests. These insects live in large communities where each helps the others.

No matter what they look like or how they live, all insects have six legs and three body parts. Here are some of the creatures you might find in your backyard. Are they insects?

Insects are all around—flying through the air, chewing on leaves, creeping through grass. Scientists think that there are more kinds of insects than there are kinds of fish or birds or any other animal in the world. Look in your own backyard and see how many insects you can find.

And always remember to count their legs!

FIND OUT MORE ABOUT INSECTS

- Make an insect calendar. On a big piece of paper, make a calendar for a week, beginning with Sunday. Each day, look for insects in your backyard and write down which ones you recognized. At the end of the week, count how many different insects you saw.

- Draw a picture of the most interesting insect you saw all week. Draw it bigger than it is. Fill up the whole piece of paper. Then tell why you found it interesting. Don't forget to count its legs as you draw your picture!

- Ask an adult to help mark off one square yard of ground in your backyard or park. Count how many insects you can find in that space. Try this in different areas—in sun, shade, grass, or dirt. Do some areas have more insects than others?

- Butterflies are among the prettiest insects. Ask an adult to help you plant a garden in your backyard or in a window box that will attract butterflies. Some flowers that butterflies are attracted to are bee balm, bougainvillea, coneflowers, geraniums, hibiscus, impatiens, marigolds, phlox, and zinnias. You can buy seeds or young plants at a nursery or gardening store. Ask the salesperson which plants will grow best where you live. Plant your garden in a sunny spot sheltered from the wind. Do not use pesticides. Place a small dish full of water in a protected spot and change the water every few days. Butterflies will be attracted to the blooming flowers and the fresh water, and you will be able to watch them all summer long. Don't try to catch your butterflies, though; their wings will be damaged if you touch them.

- You can explore the website of the Entomological Society of America for more information about insects at http://www.entsoc.org.

These are the kinds of insects and other animals that you have seen in *Bugs Are Insects*. When there is more than one creature on a page, they are listed in order from left to right.

title page:	tiger beetle
half title page:	ladybugs
page 4:	fire ant, field cricket
page 5:	mosquito, monarch butterfly, honeybee
page 6:	stinkbug, springtail, ground beetle
page 7:	giraffe weevil, picture-winged fly, eastern blue darner
page 8–9:	ladybug
page 10:	lobster
page 11:	scorpion, blue crab, shrimp
page 12:	yellowjacket
page 13:	cave cricket, Colorado potato beetle
page 14–15:	carpenter ant, ladybug
page 16–17:	garden spider
page 18:	southern stink beetle, bedbugs
page 19:	water strider
page 20–21:	ladybugs
page 22:	malaria mosquito
page 23:	birdwing butterfly
page 24:	grasshopper, lesser water boatman
page 25:	honeybee, cricket
page 26:	paper wasp
page 28:	lacewing, orb web spider, long-horned beetle, bush cricket, ladybug
page 29:	American thread-waisted wasp, flea, centipede, yellow wasp, praying mantis
page 30:	field ant, green leafhopper, firefly
page 31:	mayfly, European grasshopper, ladybug, Venus swift moth

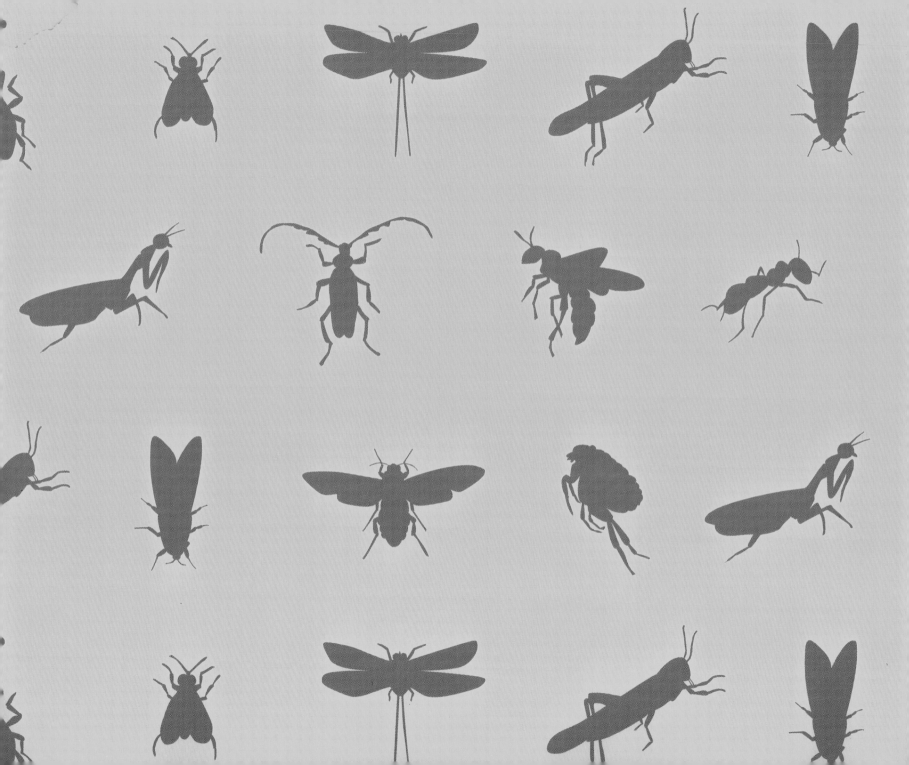